"Leading like David in a world full of Goliaths"

By

Tara Lee Davis

TARA LEE DAVIS

Copyright © 2019 Tara Lee Davis
All rights reserved.

ISBN: 978-1-946106-52-0

For sales and ordering information:
http://tdavis1141.wixsite.com/taraleedavis/blog-1
booktaraleedavis@gmail.com

Glorified Publishing
PO Box 8004
The Woodlands TX 77387
www.GlorifiedPublishing.com

Scriptures marked NIV are taken from the NEW INTERNATIONAL VERSION (NIV): Scripture taken from THE HOLY BIBLE, NEW INTERNATIONAL VERSION ®. Copyright© 1973, 1978, 1984, 2011 by Biblica, Inc.™. Used by permission of Zondervan

Scriptures marked ESV are taken from the THE HOLY BIBLE, ENGLISH STANDARD VERSION (ESV): Scriptures taken from THE HOLY BIBLE, ENGLISH STANDARD VERSION ® Copyright© 2001 by Crossway, a publishing ministry of Good News Publishers. Used by permission.

Scriptures marked TM are taken from the THE MESSAGE: THE BIBLE IN CONTEMPORARY ENGLISH (TM): Scripture taken from THE MESSAGE: THE BIBLE IN CONTEMPORARY ENGLISH, copyright©1993, 1994, 1995, 1996, 2000, 2001, 2002. Used by permission of NavPress Publishing Group

Dedication

This book and the heart behind it are dedicated to my lifelong best friend, wombmate, and better half of me, my twin sister Sara, who has fearlessly and courageously faced down every giant in her life and reminded the world that heroes do still exist. Thank you for showing me again and again what courage looks like and how to face the odds with resilience and for refusing to let me surrender to any of my giants. I am a better person because of you.

I love you, always and forever.

TARA LEE DAVIS

Foreword:

I knew God was up to something when one of my fondest moments of someone was at an evening prayer meeting. As I was walking through the sanctuary that night I walked by Tara lying prostrate on the ground. I knelt down and began to pray for her. God showed me an onion that was being peeled; it had a hard, dry layer at first but as each layer was peeled back it became soft and shiny. This may not have been the most glamorous word ever spoken over her and we laugh about it now but I can say that it has been an honor to watch God do this work in her life.

In this book, Tara lays out a path to restore true leadership back in the church and in ministries. The very nature of a leader is to walk by faith and not by sight. Leaders are never running from a battle but running to them just as David did when he faced Goliath. As a leader, God is going to ask you to take some uncalculated risks so that you can learn to trust and depend on Him. You will always be miserable trying to live a life of comfort and safety while following the status quo of Christianity. God will always ask you to raise the bar on how you live your life. He uses His leaders to create a walking, not just talking, Biblical reference of how one should live.

Today the world is full of insecure leaders that are forcing true followers of Christ to wear armor that was never meant to fit them. And in turn, we have a divided church of leaders and layman that still have a hunger to live a life that will impact the earth but not knowing what to do. This book will open many doors and hearts as a blueprint to restore the foundation of a radical, bold church. I pray it rekindles the fire of revival and starts new fires in each leader to take radical risks and advance the kingdom of Heaven.

Pastor John F. Webber

AKA "Coach"

Of the angels he says, "He makes his angels winds, and his ministers a flame of fire." Hebrews 1:7

TABLE OF CONTENTS

I: Vision: Leaders always see the big picture. Page 1

- Understanding the past is not wasted and sets the pace for our today
- Understanding the current is crucial and affects our tomorrow
- Understanding that our tomorrow is shaped by our today

II: Insecurity: Leaders refuse to let others set the limits. Page 9

- Refusing to live under the limits set by others
- Operating out of confidence in who the Lord is and what He has spoken
- Living with courage when others won't

III: Advancing: Leaders always make the first move. Page 15

- Faith without works is dead
- Being courageous and confident enough to take that first step
- Realizing that the perfect opportunity is right in front of you, not many years down the road

IV: Identity: Leaders have a firm grasp on who they are. Page 21

- The real power comes when we embrace our true identity and live that out.
- We will never be who God has created us to be when we settle for what others try to put on us.
- We can walk around in man's expectations and obligations or we can run in the freedom of who God has created us to be.

V: Momentum: Leaders always bring back the success to their team. Page 39

- Behind every great leader is a great team
- We are always better together
- Others need to see your success so they can be propelled into their destiny of giant slaying

VI: Humility: Leaders always give glory to the only One worthy. Page 45

- Every good and perfect gift is from God
- He alone gives us what we need to lead well
- Leaders clothed in humility look like Jesus, the ultimate giant slayer

VII: Cheese and Crackers: The simplicity of your everyday life. Page 51

- Leadership is not a mission to be God
- Leaders are faithful with what they've been given, no matter how small
- Leaders understand that the battles belong to the Lord and not to them

VIII: Conclusion: Questions for Reflection. Page 55

Acknowledgments

Writing a book is never a solo accomplishment. It takes an incredible team of selfless people to birth something so special. My mere words of gratitude will never adequately express the true thankfulness I feel for each one of these incredible teammates.

I'd like to thank my twin sister Sara for constantly praying me through and encouraging me. She knew when I wanted to quit, long before I spoke the words. She read through countless drafts, giving wise feedback and new insight. This book would not exist without her reminding me again and again to "refuse to let these giants win." Thank you, Sis, for always being my biggest fan.

I need to say thank you to my Texas family, the Crisps and Rojos. This time away in the snowy cabin of New Mexico has brought this book from a pile of dust and discouragement to a living, breathing thing while your friendship has softened this hard, little heart into one full of life again. Thank you for always seeing the best in me and loving me at my worst.

Thank you to John, aka Coach, for writing the foreword to this book. I started learning how to fearlessly face my giants with courage the day I met you and your family. You and Misty have had such an impact in my walk with Jesus, and I'm deeply grateful.

To my tribe, thank you for the countless laughs, tears, meals shared, cards played, and memories made in this season. You remind me again and again that we are better together.

Edie, my publisher…it is pure joy to work with you! Thank you for your professionalism and your passion for Jesus and Kingdom.

Most importantly, thank you to the only One worth mentioning, Jesus

Christ. All credit and accolades and glory belong to You. You have been faithful when I was not and You have loved me enough to refuse to leave me stuck. My only hope and prayer in life are to make much of You. I pray You'll find me faithful until my last breath. Thank You for being far bigger and stronger than any giants in my life!

Introduction

Everyone loves an underdog story, especially when the odds are stacked against him and yet, even so, he still comes out on top. Some of the classics of all time have been such heroic storylines as Anne Franke and her diary of desperate hope in the midst of such fierce and rampant hatred; Cliff Young and his world record finish of an ultramarathon, 544 endless miles of pure agony when the only backer he had was what he believed about himself; and Louie Zamperini and his enduring faith and perseverance in the midst of life's fiercest storms. Who doesn't love a story that proves that anything is possible to those who simply believe?

Of all such stories that exist in the world, my all-time favorite is David and Goliath. Ever since I was a child, my eyes would light up when my faithful Sunday school teachers (God bless the ones who keep showing up week after week!) would use the felt boards and take us on a journey through the adventure. I love that we can read the same story from Scripture again and again and through the power and guidance and wisdom of the Holy Spirit, He can show us things we've never seen before. That is where this book was birthed: from the Holy Spirit's influence and the everyday life I've lived, through which I am learning to dance with grace. My hope and prayer are that this book will inspire you to find your inner David and in so doing, lead the ones in your camp to victory in and through Christ Jesus!

1 Samuel 17 English Standard Version (ESV)

David and Goliath

17 Now the Philistines gathered their armies for battle. And they were gathered at Socoh, which belongs to Judah, and encamped between Socoh and Azekah, in Ephes-dammim. ²And Saul and the men of Israel were gathered, and encamped in the Valley of Elah, and drew up in line of battle against the Philistines. ³And the Philistines stood on the mountain on the one side, and Israel stood on the mountain on the other side, with a valley between them. ⁴And there came out from the camp of the Philistines a champion named Goliath of Gath, whose height was six[a] cubits[b] and a span. ⁵He had a helmet of bronze on his head, and he was armed with a coat of mail, and the weight of the coat was five thousand shekels[c] of bronze. ⁶And he had bronze armor on his legs, and a javelin of bronze slung between his shoulders. ⁷The shaft of his spear was like a weaver's beam, and his spear's head weighed six hundred shekels of iron. And his shield-bearer went before him. ⁸He stood and shouted to the ranks of Israel, "Why have you come out to draw up for battle? Am I not a Philistine, and are you not servants of Saul? Choose a man for yourselves, and let him come down to me. ⁹If he is able to fight with me and kill me, then we will be your servants. But if I prevail against him and kill him, then you shall be our servants and serve us." ¹⁰And the Philistine said, "I defy the ranks of Israel this day. Give me a man, that we may fight together." ¹¹When Saul and all Israel heard these words of the Philistine, they were dismayed and greatly afraid.

¹²Now David was the son of an Ephrathite of Bethlehem in

Judah, named Jesse, who had eight sons. In the days of Saul the man was already old and advanced in years.[d] ¹³ The three oldest sons of Jesse had followed Saul to the battle. And the names of his three sons who went to the battle were Eliab the firstborn, and next to him Abinadab, and the third Shammah. ¹⁴ David was the youngest. The three eldest followed Saul, ¹⁵ but David went back and forth from Saul to feed his father's sheep at Bethlehem. ¹⁶ For forty days the Philistine came forward and took his stand, morning and evening.

¹⁷ And Jesse said to David his son, "Take for your brothers an ephah[e] of this parched grain, and these ten loaves, and carry them quickly to the camp to your brothers. ¹⁸ Also take these ten cheeses to the commander of their thousand. See if your brothers are well, and bring some token from them."

¹⁹ Now Saul and they and all the men of Israel were in the Valley of Elah, fighting with the Philistines. ²⁰ And David rose early in the morning and left the sheep with a keeper and took the provisions and went, as Jesse had commanded him. And he came to the encampment as the host was going out to the battle line, shouting the war cry. ²¹ And Israel and the Philistines drew up for battle, army against army. ²² And David left the things in charge of the keeper of the baggage and ran to the ranks and went and greeted his brothers. ²³ As he talked with them, behold, the champion, the Philistine of Gath, Goliath by name, came up out of the ranks of the Philistines and spoke the same words as before. And David heard him.

²⁴ All the men of Israel, when they saw the man, fled from him and were much afraid. ²⁵ And the men of Israel said, "Have you seen this man who has come up? Surely he has come up to defy Israel. And the king will enrich the man who kills him with great riches and will give

him his daughter and make his father's house free in Israel." ²⁶ And David said to the men who stood by him, "What shall be done for the man who kills this Philistine and takes away the reproach from Israel? For who is this uncircumcised Philistine, that he should defy the armies of the living God?" ²⁷ And the people answered him in the same way, "So shall it be done to the man who kills him."

²⁸ Now Eliab his eldest brother heard when he spoke to the men. And Eliab's anger was kindled against David, and he said, "Why have you come down? And with whom have you left those few sheep in the wilderness? I know your presumption and the evil of your heart, for you have come down to see the battle." ²⁹ And David said, "What have I done now? Was it not but a word?" ³⁰ And he turned away from him toward another, and spoke in the same way, and the people answered him again as before.

³¹ When the words that David spoke were heard, they repeated them before Saul, and he sent for him. ³² And David said to Saul, "Let no man's heart fail because of him. Your servant will go and fight with this Philistine." ³³ And Saul said to David, "You are not able to go against this Philistine to fight with him, for you are but a youth, and he has been a man of war from his youth." ³⁴ But David said to Saul, "Your servant used to keep sheep for his father. And when there came a lion, or a bear, and took a lamb from the flock, ³⁵ I went after him and struck him and delivered it out of his mouth. And if he arose against me, I caught him by his beard and struck him and killed him. ³⁶ Your servant has struck down both lions and bears, and this uncircumcised Philistine shall be like one of them, for he has defied the armies of the living God." ³⁷ And David said, "The LORD who delivered me from the paw of the lion and from the paw of the bear will deliver me from the hand of this Philistine." And Saul said to

David, "Go, and the LORD be with you!"

[38] Then Saul clothed David with his armor. He put a helmet of bronze on his head and clothed him with a coat of mail, [39] and David strapped his sword over his armor. And he tried in vain to go, for he had not tested them. Then David said to Saul, "I cannot go with these, for I have not tested them." So David put them off. [40] Then he took his staff in his hand and chose five smooth stones from the brook and put them in his shepherd's pouch. His sling was in his hand, and he approached the Philistine.

[41] And the Philistine moved forward and came near to David, with his shield-bearer in front of him. [42] And when the Philistine looked and saw David, he disdained him, for he was but a youth, ruddy and handsome in appearance. [43] And the Philistine said to David, "Am I a dog, that you come to me with sticks?" And the Philistine cursed David by his gods. [44] The Philistine said to David, "Come to me, and I will give your flesh to the birds of the air and to the beasts of the field." [45] Then David said to the Philistine, "You come to me with a sword and with a spear and with a javelin, but I come to you in the name of the LORD of hosts, the God of the armies of Israel, whom you have defied. [46] This day the LORD will deliver you into my hand, and I will strike you down and cut off your head. And I will give the dead bodies of the host of the Philistines this day to the birds of the air and to the wild beasts of the earth, that all the earth may know that there is a God in Israel, [47] and that all this assembly may know that the LORD saves not with sword and spear. For the battle is the LORD's, and he will give you into our hand."

[48] When the Philistine arose and came and drew near to meet David, David ran quickly toward the battle line to meet the Philistine. [49] And

David put his hand in his bag and took out a stone and slung it and struck the Philistine on his forehead. The stone sank into his forehead, and he fell on his face to the ground.

⁵⁰ So David prevailed over the Philistine with a sling and with a stone, and struck the Philistine and killed him. There was no sword in the hand of David. ⁵¹ Then David ran and stood over the Philistine and took his sword and drew it out of its sheath and killed him and cut off his head with it. When the Philistines saw that their champion was dead, they fled. ⁵² And the men of Israel and Judah rose with a shout and pursued the Philistines as far as Gath[i] and the gates of Ekron, so that the wounded Philistines fell on the way from Shaaraim as far as Gath and Ekron. ⁵³ And the people of Israel came back from chasing the Philistines, and they plundered their camp. ⁵⁴ And David took the head of the Philistine and brought it to Jerusalem, but he put his armor in his tent.

⁵⁵ As soon as Saul saw David go out against the Philistine, he said to Abner, the commander of the army, "Abner, whose son is this youth?" And Abner said, "As your soul lives, O king, I do not know." ⁵⁶ And the king said, "Inquire whose son the boy is." ⁵⁷ And as soon as David returned from the striking down of the Philistine, Abner took him, and brought him before Saul with the head of the Philistine in his hand. ⁵⁸ And Saul said to him, "Whose son are you, young man?" And David answered, "I am the son of your servant Jesse the Bethlehemite."

TARA LEE DAVIS

def·i·ni·tions

sav·age

- not domesticated or under human control
- fierce, ferocious
- wild, uncultivated

Go·li·ath

- a Philistine champion who was killed by David in I Samuel 17
- giant

Da·vid

- a Hebrew shepherd who became the second king of Israel in succession to Saul according to biblical accounts

- underdog

lead·er

- a person who has commanding authority or influence

I
Vision

"Vision is the art of seeing what is invisible to others."

Jonathan Swift

TARA LEE DAVIS

"If people can't see what God is doing, they stumble all over themselves; But when they attend to what he reveals, they are most blessed."

Proverbs 29:18 (The Message Bible)

Helen Keller said once, "The only thing worse than being blind is having sight but no vision." Vision is the art of what we see; it often goes beyond our physical eyes and into the eyes of our soul. Our perspective is inherently shaped by our vision, what we spend our time gazing upon: the dreams, the plans, the goals, the vision.

It's the vision of a young scholar to become a renowned doctor that keeps him studying until the sun peeks over the horizon in those first hushed, holy moments of each new day. It's the vision of record-breaking that compels the young athlete to press in and endure, even in the midst of a setback, to keep pushing and striving. It's the vision of a single mother, juggling her full-time work and part-time school and full-time parenting to provide a better life for her children that inspires her to keep loving, learning and growing.

The ones who often succeed the most in life are the ones pregnant with vision, waiting to birth their dreams into reality and inspire the world around them. But what exactly is vision, and how does one embrace it in his every-day, ordinary life?

Find a great leader and you'll find he has vision. Great leaders have vision that is far bigger and greater than them. Great vision is simply this: understanding that our yesterday affected our today and our today will most certainly shape our tomorrow. When a leader has a vision, he has something - a goal, a dream - that he is working towards. But like anything else in life, it's not a quick fix.

A great leader isn't just given a vision in one brief moment, simply to accomplish it the next day. That is not how vision works. Vision is a growing, a becoming, a shaping, a birthing. It's a complex creation that is birthed out of the details of our lives that, frankly, at the moment and time of happening, seem small and insignificant at best. However, great leaders are able to embrace every detail of their lives and steward them in such a way that it helps birth the vision into reality.

David was the youngest of eight sons to Jesse and spent his early years in the fields with his sheep. Sheep are at the complete mercy of their environments and predators, so in order to survive, they need someone skilled enough to not only navigate unknown territory but fierce enough to fend off any potential predators.

This was the exact setup for David. He would spend the first part of his life navigating unknown territory and fending off fierce predators from the flock. I've often wondered if young David knew how this would play out in the later years of his life, or was it, perhaps, just another ordinary day? The shepherds were responsible for making sure their flock was fed, watered, exercised, and maintained good health. This often-times meant long days of traveling by foot through adverse weather conditions and even longer nights, keeping watch over the flock.

Somewhere between the ages of ten and thirteen, David was anointed to be the next king by the prophet Samuel, found in 1 Samuel 16. As

the youngest of seven brothers, I'd imagine there was no celebration or knuckle rubs on the head, only subtle jealousy that seeped through like a poison. It was in these moments, moments that called for great celebration and honor that were replaced with jealousy and a stiff silence, that would begin to shape the heart of young David for the rejection that he would face later on in life. Upon being anointed, life resumed as normal for David until a few years later when he was summoned to play melodies on his harp for the mad king. Then, some years later, life took a major turn.

In the Valley of Elah, the Philistines were drawn up on one side and God's people, the Israelites, were on the opposite hillside. The advantage of the Israelites was that God was on their side. The advantage of the Philistines was their giant, Goliath. Goliath stood at a towering nine feet and nine inches tall. As if his impressive height was not enough, he sported one hundred twenty-five pounds of armor and carried a spear that was like a weaver's beam whose tip alone weighed another fifteen pounds. For forty days, this giant came out and taunted the Israelite army. In response, for forty days, the Israelites stood there, shaking in fear at the battle line, unable to move.

During this war, Jesse was old and concerned about his three oldest sons off at war. So he did what any good father would do: he sent thirty-six pounds of roasted grain and ten loaves of bread with his youngest, David, instructing him to go check on his brothers. Again, was this just another day in the life of young David? At this point in his life journey, he was between fifteen and seventeen years old. But David was faithful and did as his father had asked because great leaders are faithful with the small long before they are faithful with the big.

David approached the camp and delivered the grain and bread as promised when everything changed. The same giant, Goliath, came out taunting the people of God, making fun of them, and it set David off. David couldn't understand why anyone would allow someone to not only make fun of God's people, but to make fun of God Himself! The story escalated at this point and for once there was excitement in the camp. David decided that if no one else was willing to do anything, then he, in fact, would.

David's brothers, in a typical big brother fashion, urged their brother to, "go home, because you don't belong here." Others were in shock; some questioned the size of David, and I'm sure there were still others who were relieved that someone else would step up and do the job they had no desire to do. King Saul then offered David his armor, but in his wisdom, even at a young age, David politely declined because he knew that great leaders can never run in someone else's armor but must walk in their own destiny.

However, here was the clincher for vision: David understood that every detail of his life up until this point had set the perfect backdrop for his victory!

> *But David said to Saul, "Your servant has been keeping his father's sheep. When a lion or a bear came and carried off a sheep from the flock, I went after it, struck it and rescued the sheep from its mouth. When it turned on me, I seized it by its hair, struck it and killed it. Your servant has killed both the lion and the bear; this uncircumcised Philistine will be like one of them, because he has defied the armies of the living God. The LORD who rescued me from the paw of the lion and the paw of the bear will rescue me from the hand of this Philistine." Saul said to David, "Go, and the LORD be with you."* I Samuel 17:34-37

As a teenager, David was able to reconcile his past as a means to not only change the trajectory of his today but also directly impacted his tomorrows. The beauty of this principle is found in that not only did this benefit him as an individual, but it also benefited countless others.

When it comes to the Kingdom of God and His story being woven within ours, we must understand and embrace that nothing is wasted. Great leaders always understand that our past is not wasted when placed within God's hands, but that our today is crucial and directly affects our tomorrow. Great leaders don't sit back and wait for history to repeat itself or change, but they take every piece of their journey and use it, not only for the good of themselves but for those around them.

The mundane becomes miraculous when we place it in God's hands and become good stewards of not only the time allotted us but the life experiences we have endured. When we run with vision in our hearts, our moments are not wasted, but in fact fuel the drive in us to be incredible leaders. Leaders without vision are as effective as ships without rudders.

TARA LEE DAVIS

II
Insecurity

"Since it is so likely that children will meet cruel enemies, let them at least have heard of brave knights and heroic courage."

C.S. Lewis

TARA LEE DAVIS

"Do not be anxious about anything, but in every situation, by prayer and petition, with thanksgiving, present your request to God."

Philippians 4:6

We've all been there before, awkwardly standing in line, waiting to be picked for a team. Our palms sweat, hearts raced and our minds reeled with a million *what-ifs* all at once. It was almost too much for anyone to endure, especially on the playground in the middle of a school day. I believe the most wasted use of power in our society today is our words. I love how The Message translation says it in Proverbs 18:21, "Words kill you, words kill life; they're either poison or fruit-you choose." Every single human on the planet struggles with insecurity, and if we trace it back to its root, more often than not, we'll find that our insecurities were first spoken over us with words.

As leaders we have far more influence than we realize. The way in which we carry ourselves, our presence, whether we are fully there or just partially there as well as how we lead all alter the atmospheres in which we find ourselves. It is the responsibility of a great leader to not only create cultures and climates that promote confidence but to also lead from a place of confidence rather than insecurity.

First, great leaders refuse to live under the limits set by others. Remember when David refused the king's armor? David knew he was created to run the destiny set out for him by God, not stumble around in the expectations (armor) of man. It's so interesting that we give so much power to what others think of or speak about us. When did humans have that much power? They have that much power when we give it to them. We struggle to believe what God says about us, and when we do that we often "exchange the truth of God for a lie" according to Romans 1:25. And as the rest of that verse explains, when you and I choose to believe what others say about us over what God says about us, we worship created things rather than the Creator. This is not how we were created or designed to live!

David no doubt faced limitations. His own family didn't exactly vouch for him. There's no mention of a party with cake and ice cream to celebrate his anointing as king at such a young age. In fact, he was going to be passed over had it not been for the tender whisper of God to the prophet Samuel to ask if there were any other sons. *"More? Oh yeah, but he's just out with the sheep in the field."* No big deal. Shoulder shrugging was what accompanied conversations about David from early on. Maybe you, too, can relate.

So when David showed up that day with those thirty-six pounds of roasted grain and ten loaves of bread, King Saul wanted him to wear his armor. At first glance, that may seem kind of the king. But if we pause and really consider what we're looking at it here, it was nothing more than a lame pat on the back. That armor was specifically sized for King Saul, who compared with a teenage boy, was certainly larger. Not only would David not truly be protected, but he would no doubt be made to look like a fool. He could not run in that armor. If David had worn the king's armor, David would have lived under the expectations of someone else. And the danger with that is this - we can either live in the expectations of God or the expectations of man, but we cannot do both. It's impossible. David would have stumbled in that armor, but David knew that he needed to run into what God was calling him to do.

> *"Then Saul dressed David in his own tunic. He put a coat of armor on him and a bronze helmet on his head. David fastened on his sword over the tunic and tried walking around because he was not used to them. "I cannot go in these," he said to Saul, "because I am not used to them." So*

he took them off.[40] *Then he took his staff in his hand, chose five smooth stones from the stream, put them in the pouch of his shepherd's bag and, with his sling in his hand, approached the Philistine."* (1 Samuel 17:38-40)

God has created each of us uniquely. With billions of people on this tiny blue dot that keeps circling the sun, it's fascinating that every single human has a different set of fingerprints. We are all hard-wired with unique personality traits, gifts and assets, strengths and weaknesses. When it comes to leadership, why do we think that we need to fit a cookie cutter mold? David understood this and refused to be held back by what others thought of him or even suggested for him.

Great leaders operate out of confidence in who God is and what He has spoken, period. Why are we more familiar with what others speak or think of us instead of what God has spoken? Think about that for a moment. Chances are you've got a pretty good idea of the opinions of others, but do you know all that God says about you? When was the last time you wrote down the promises of God over your life? When was the last time you squared up with yourself in the mirror and spoke the truth over your heart? Great leaders understand that while others may speak negatively, what really matters is what God speaks.

And lastly, great leaders will live and lead with courage, even

when others won't. Forty days…that's nine-hundred sixty hours, which equates to fifty-seven thousand, six hundred minutes of standing. That is how long the Israelites stood on the line of battle, being taunted day in and day out by the Philistines and their great champion Goliath.

What did it take? A well-trained army? Check. Weapons of every kind? Check. Strong men to lead the charge? Check. Well strategized battle plans? Check. The one thing the Israelites lacked David had, and that one thing was courage. Nelson Mandela said, "*I learned that courage was not the absence of fear, but the triumph over it. The brave man is not he who does not feel afraid, but he who conquers fear.*" The Israelites lacked courage because they cared more about what Goliath said instead of what God had said. David, however, was the exact opposite. David was so offended by what Goliath said that he would stop at nothing to take him down.

David had every reason to lead from a place of insecurity. His brothers mocked him, the king questioned him, and the people doubted him. Yet, David knew what God had spoken because, in every season of his life up until this point, David spent time with God and learned His Word while tending his flock. David's confidence soared because his foundation was solid truth. And when you stand upon what's true, then it simply does not matter what the enemy may throw at you.

I have often thought about how the story would have ended had David succumbed to his own insecurities. No doubt the battle would have lasted at least another forty days and insecurities would have grown stronger. That's what happens when there is no truth - the lies and insecurities grow. Where there is no courage there is only fear. Great leaders will lead from a place of pure confidence: confidence in who God is and what He has spoken. This will give them the courage needed to face whatever giant is taunting the rest of the camp.

III

Advancing

"Isn't it funny how day by day nothing changes, but when you look back, everything is different."

C.S. Lewis

TARA LEE DAVIS

"There is a time for everything, and a season for every activity under the heavens."

Ecclesiastes 3:1

I remember standing on the block of the pool, my toes barely hanging over the edge of the rough platform. Middle school had been awkward on every level, and then I found myself in a super starchy, thicker than wool, three sizes too small, one-piece swimsuit which had likely been at the school since its inception "thousands" of years ago.

"I can do all thing through Jesus Christ who gives me strength," (Philippians 4:13) kept playing through my head, almost in sync with my sporadically beating heart that was racing long before I ever broke the surface of the over-chlorinated water. It was my swimming test, and today was the day. The goal? Dive in, swim down and back… and all without drowning, quitting, or getting eaten some flesh eating amoeba that was surely lurking in the frozen depths below.

I was entirely paralyzed by my own fear, and what did I gain by waiting to take that first leap? Nothing, absolutely nothing. As a matter of fact, that fear not only held me back but inhibited my best, I was so flustered by the time I took that first leap that I ended up unofficially winning the belly flop contest that everyone else had avoided participating in.

That's what fear does; it cripples, paralyzes, and haunts us. Hebrews 11:1 states, "Without faith, it is impossible to please God." But fear is what squelches out our faith. So instead of doing the thing, instead of stepping out in courage and obedience, we are paralyzed in our fear.

Our faith, inevitably, is dead. How many people do we know that are not living their best life? They seem held back, their wasted potential withering away with the passing of each day. Great leaders don't wait for the right time ... great leaders act when action is required.

There is a thing within the field of photography that is referred to as the golden hour. The *golden hour* is the period of daytime that occurs shortly after sunrise or before sunset. At this particular time of day, the light is redder and softer than when the sun is higher in the sky. Apparently, this golden hour creates the perfect backdrop for stunning photographs.

Interestingly enough, "the golden hour" is also a term within the medical field: the first hour after the occurrence of a traumatic injury. Medically speaking, the golden hour is considered the most critical timing for successful surgical intervention. One term, two different fields, and two very different approaches; both with an urgent sense of timing but one for the creation of beauty and wonder and the other for the saving of life.

I believe this is how we approach life: our daily activities, our mindsets and mentalities, the way we face challenges, and the way we handle our demands and responsibilities. The child who cleans his room because he enjoys an orderly environment will rarely need nagging; however, the child who cleans his room in an effort to save his life from his over-exasperated mother will likely need nagging again and again. Whatever manner we approach life with will directly affect the outcome. Great leaders not only understand this but embrace this in their everyday decisions.

I've thought often about David's to-do list. I'm convinced that it was not on his agenda of the day to slay a giant. This was not a bucket list item; a dream, or even something a life coach had advised him to pursue. His mission was simple: take the snacks from Pops and check on his brothers. Did he accomplish that task? Yes. Was he obedient? Yes. Did he stay faithful with the small? Yes. But it was in his every day, ordinary life that God would use David to rewrite the history books forever!

David lived with a sense of wonder…just read the Psalms. The young lad put more of his heart into everyday life than anyone I know. Fully alive, fully aware, fully living his best life, even in the midst of life's deepest, darkest valleys. It's no wonder then that when David heard the gnarly giant making fun of God and His people that he didn't shy away from the conflict or demand an answer as to who would get rid of this towering, taunting tease. He made the first move, he took that first step, he signed up long before anyone passed him an ink pen to sign his name on the dotted line.

What lies ahead of you today? What is the one thing you keep avoiding? What has God asked you to do, again and again, that you keep pushing to the bottom of the pile? Your perfect moment is now, your golden hour is here. It's far better to lead from a place of wonder before you find yourself leading from a place of crisis. Opportunities don't fall into place, they are everyday moments that are seized by the greats among us. Will you be confident and courageous enough to leap off? Or will you miss your golden hour and in so doing lose your life? Dramatic? Perhaps, though I've lingered long on the possibility of David missing that moment. How would the story have ended?

There were several years of my life that I pursued becoming an amateur boxer. I was fascinated with the sport and read books, watched training videos, watched fights, and even spoke with a woman who owned a local boxing gym. I was committed, hitting my bag daily and would even have weekly fights with friends in which we found ourselves sparring into the late-night hours. I loved the sport and I was willing to work for it. I remember my coach, who also happened to be my pastor, told me something profound one day, and it was one of those moments that marked me. He told me that the most dangerous fighter is the unpredictable fighter; the one who throws a hard upper-cut when his opponent expects him to be hovering in the corner. The unpredictable fighter sets the pace, switches up the footwork, refuses to fall into a rhythm or pattern that would be far too easy for the opponent to read. The unpredictable fighter doesn't fight defensively, merely reacting to what has been done to them; rather, the most dangerous fighter fights offensively, setting the pace of the fight.

Great leaders are unpredictable fighters. They're the ones who keep dreaming when everyone else has stopped. They are the ones who keep serving, refusing to bow down to an egotistical, proud and self-preserving culture that runs so rampant today. Great leaders keep showing up, taking that first move, and stepping up to lead and serve in ways that others refuse to do.

IV

Identity

"Define yourself as one radically loved by God. This is your true self; every other identity is an illusion."

Brennan Manning

TARA LEE DAVIS

> ***"Behold, I have engraved you on the palms of my hands; your walls are continually before me."***

Isaiah 49:16

As a child, masks were fun. As an adult, masks are confusing. A child's imagination is fascinating, with their ability to create, invent, dream, and live in these faraway lands. My twin sister and I were best friends even before we were born, and my most favorite childhood memories include playing in our fort between the two crooked pine trees out front. My sister and I could come up with the wildest stories and would lose track of time long before we lost track of any wild good chase ideas or epic adventures. And yet, how many of us grew up behind a different set of masks? We long to be known, to be seen, to be loved just as we are and yet we lack the courage to take the masks off.

Great leaders have a firm grasp on who they are. They refuse to be defined or devalued by anyone or anything else because they know who they are and whose they are. They were a child of God long before they were someone's spouse, they were a sinner in need of grace long before they were a chief executive officer. We will never be who God has created us to be when we settle for what others put on us; or, when we prefer to play pretend as grown adults rather than be who God has called and created us to be.

David had a lot to live under. The youngest with seven older brothers, the sheepherder, the pooper scooper; the one called last for the possible anointing as king, the one with whom the king was so enraged there was a death sentence on his back; the short one, the young one, the delivery boy, the one everyone doubted, the one the king questioned, the one for whom there was no armor sized just right. There were plenty of masks and insecurities for David to hide behind.

But what most would see as a curse was actually a pivotal blessing and promotion for David. He spent the majority of his early life in the fields, on the rocky terrain of mountains, in the middle of a valley in a downpour, with just him, his flock, and the Great Shepherd. Were the days filled with the melodies of life? Yes, but they were also filled with the Father's voice, God tenderly speaking over David who he was. This created the firmest foundation possible for any young man and set him up for incredible success later on in his life. At a young age, David embraced who he truly was as a child of God and he tapped into his power when he lived that out.

Great leaders refuse to stumble around in the expectations or obligations of others. How many times in a typical week do you feel burdened by the expectations of others? We all know how frustrating that is. The unrealistic and often unfair expectations of others weigh us down and are perhaps one of the most exhausting cycles we find ourselves trapped in. Yet, how often do you and I place expectations on others?

I think it's fair and healthy to have a certain set of standard expectations that are non-negotiables: Love, respect, honesty, etc. But there have been times when I've been disappointed in or frustrated with a friend, but when I pause long enough to think it through, the reality is I had an unfair expectation of that particular friend.

David was faced with plenty of opportunities to fall prey to the expectations of others. He could have gone home, just like his big brothers advised. He could have believed the king and changed his mind about fighting Goliath. He could have wavered in unbelief and faltered in fear. But David, the great leader that he was, embraced who he was as a child of God and ran into his destiny.

Do you know who you are? Most of us would answer that question with a name and follow it up with any number of labels such as mother, father, brother, doctor, teacher, etc. While those things are certainly markers of us, descriptors even, they do not define us. The only thing or person that has the power and wisdom to define us is our beginning, and for every single human on the planet, our beginning is a really big God who took the time to create us with His hands. Whether you believe in God or not, this is your beginning. And your identity, your truest self, traces back to what He spoke of you because He is the One who not only designed you but actually knit you together in your mother's womb.

Maybe you need to be reminded of who you are. Maybe you've never been told. Below are truths about who you are and great leaders embrace these as their own. I think one of the most powerful things anyone can do is to look ourselves in the eye each morning and speak the Word of God over ourselves. I AM was the name of God long before it was a label you used to identify yourself with. And everything that comes from your mouth following those two words not only "defines" you but also labels God. For example, if I say "I am stupid," I am not only speaking a lie over myself but over God as well.

I've enclosed a list below, along with references, that you can use to realign yourself to your truest self. This is not an exhaustive list as Scripture is filled with many more truths about who we are. May these truths permeate through every mask you've ever worn, may they shatter every lie you've ever believed, and may they strip you of any false words spoken over you. It will be difficult, yes. But just because you don't believe it to be true does not mean it's not true. There is power in the things you speak.

Who I Am Declarations

I am a child of God.

The Spirit himself bears witness with our spirit that we are children of God.

Romans 8:16

I am redeemed from the hand of the enemy.

Let the redeemed of the LORD say so, whom he has redeemed from trouble.

Psalm 107:2

I am forgiven.

He has delivered us from the domain of darkness and transferred us to the kingdom of his beloved Son, in whom we have redemption, the forgiveness of sins.

Colossians 1:13-14

I am saved by grace through faith.

For by grace you have been saved through faith. And this is not your own doing; it is the gift of God.

Ephesians 2:8

I am justified.

Therefore, since we have been justified by faith, we[a] have peace with God through our Lord Jesus Christ.

Romans 5:1

I am sanctified.

And such were some of you. But you were washed, you were sanctified, you were justified in the name of the Lord Jesus Christ and by the Spirit of our God.

1 Corinthians 6:11

I am a new creature.

Therefore, if anyone is in Christ, he is a new creation.[a] The old has passed away; behold, the new has come.

2 Corinthians 5:17

I am a partaker of His divine nature.

By which he has granted to us his precious and very great promises, so that through them you may become partakers of the divine nature, having escaped from the corruption that is in the world because of sinful desire.

2 Peter 1:4

I am redeemed from the curse of the law.

Christ redeemed us from the curse of the law by becoming a curse for us—for it is written, "Cursed is everyone who is hanged on a tree"—

Galatians 3:13

I am delivered from the power of darkness.

He has delivered us from the domain of darkness and transferred us to the kingdom of his beloved Son.

Colossians 1:13

I am led by the Spirit of God.

For all who are led by the Spirit of God are sons[a] of God.
Romans 8:14

I am free from all bondage.

So if the Son sets you free, you will be free indeed.
John 8:36

I am kept in safety wherever I go.

For he will command his angels concerning you to guard you in all your ways.
Psalm 91:11

I am getting all of my needs met by Jesus.

And my God will supply every need of yours according to his riches in glory in Christ Jesus.

Philippians 4:19

I am casting all of my cares on Jesus.

...casting all your anxieties on him, because he cares for you.

1 Peter 5:7

I am strong in the Lord and in the power of His might.

Finally, be strong in the Lord and in the strength of his might.

Ephesians 6:10

I am doing all things through Christ who strengthens me.

I can do all things through him who strengthens me.

Philippians 4:13

I am an heir of God and a joint heir with Jesus.

And if children, then heirs—heirs of God and fellow heirs with Christ, provided we suffer with him in order that we may also be glorified with him.

Romans 8:17

I am observing and doing the Lord's commandments.

The LORD will open to you his good treasury, the heavens, to give the rain to your land in its season and to bless all the work of your hands. And you shall lend to many nations, but you shall not borrow.

Deuteronomy 28:12

I am blessed coming in and blessed going out.

Blessed shall you be when you come in, and blessed shall you be when you go out.

Deuteronomy 28:6

I am an heir of eternal life.

And this is the testimony, that God gave us eternal life, and this life is in his Son. Whoever has the Son has life; whoever does not have the Son of God does not have life.

1 John 5:11-12

I am blessed with all spiritual blessings.

Blessed be the God and Father of our Lord Jesus Christ, who has blessed us in Christ with every spiritual blessing in the heavenly places.

Ephesians 1:3

I am healed by His stripes.

He himself bore our sins in his body on the tree, that we might die to sin and live to righteousness. By his wounds you have been healed.

1 Peter 2:24

I am exercising my authority over the enemy.

Behold, I have given you authority to tread on serpents and scorpions, and over all the power of the enemy, and nothing shall hurt you.

Luke 10:19

I am above only and not beneath.

And the LORD will make you the head and not the tail, and you shall only go up and not down, if you obey the commandments of the LORD your God, which I command you today, being careful to do them.

Deuteronomy 28:13

I am more than a conqueror.

No, in all these things we are more than conquerors through him who loved us.

Romans 8:37

I am establishing God's Word here on Earth.

I will give you the keys of the kingdom of heaven, and whatever you bind on earth shall be bound in heaven, and whatever you loose on earth shall be loosed[a] in heaven."

Matthew 16:19

I am an overcomer by the blood of the Lamb and the word of my testimony.

And they have conquered him by the blood of the Lamb and by the word of their testimony, for they loved not their lives even unto death.

Revelation 12:11

I am daily overcoming the devil.

Little children, you are from God and have overcome them, for he who is in you is greater than he who is in the world.

I John 4:4

I am not moved by what I see.

as we look not to the things that are seen but to the things that are unseen. For the things that are seen are transient, but the things that are unseen are eternal.

2 Corinthians 4:18

I am walking by faith and not by sight.

For we walk by faith, not by sight.

2 Corinthians 5:7

I am bringing every thought into captivity.

We destroy arguments and every lofty opinion raised against the knowledge of God and take every thought captive to obey Christ.

2 Corinthians 10:5

I am being transformed by renewing my mind.

I appeal to you therefore, brothers,[a] by the mercies of God, to present your bodies as a living sacrifice, holy and acceptable to God, which is your spiritual worship.[b] Do not be conformed to this world,[c] but be transformed by the renewal of your mind, that by testing you may discern what is the will of God, what is good and acceptable and perfect.

Romans 12:2

I am reigning in life through Christ Jesus.

For if, because of one man's trespass, death reigned through that one man, much more will those who receive the abundance of grace and the free gift of righteousness reign in life through the one man Jesus Christ.

Romans 5:17

I am the righteousness of God in Christ.

For our sake he made him to be sin who knew no sin, so that in him we might become the righteousness of God.

2 Corinthians 5:21

I am an imitator of Jesus.

Therefore be imitators of God, as beloved children.

Ephesians 5:1

I am the light of the world.

You are the light of the world. A city set on a hill cannot be hidden.

Matthew 5:14

I am blessing the Lord at all times and continually praising the Lord with my mouth.

I will bless the LORD at all times; his praise shall continually be in my mouth.

Psalm 34:1

I am loved by God.

"For God so loved the world,[a] that he gave his only Son, that whoever believes in him should not perish but have eternal life."

John 3:16

I am forgiven.

In whom we have redemption, the forgiveness of sins.

Colossians 1:14

I am saved by grace through faith.

For by grace you have been saved through faith. And this is not your own doing; it is the gift of God.

Ephesians 2:8

I am loving God with all of my heart, soul, mind and strength.

And he said to him, "You shall love the Lord your God with all your heart and with all your soul and with all your mind.

Matthew 22:37

I am delivered from the power of darkness.

He has delivered us from the domain of darkness and transferred us to the kingdom of his beloved Son.

Colossians 1:13

I am praying without ceasing.

Pray without ceasing.

1 Thessalonians 5:17

I am created in His image.

For those whom he foreknew he also predestined to be conformed to the image of his Son, in order that he might be the firstborn among many brothers.

Romans 8:29

I am abiding in His love.

So we have come to know and to believe the love that God has for us. God is love, and whoever abides in love abides in God, and God abides in him.

1 John 4:16

I am free from fear.

There is no fear in love, but perfect love casts out fear. For fear has to do with punishment, and whoever fears has not been perfected in love.

1 John 4:18

I am increasing in the knowledge of God.

so as to walk in a manner worthy of the Lord, fully pleasing to him: bearing fruit in every good work and increasing in the knowledge of God;

Colossians 1:10

I am fully convinced that what God has promised He is able to perform.

fully convinced that God was able to do what he had promised.

Romans 4:21

I am wearing God's armor.

Finally, be strong in the Lord and in the strength of his might. Put on the whole armor of God, that you may be able to stand against the schemes of the devil. For we do not wrestle against flesh and blood, but against the rulers, against the authorities, against the cosmic powers over this present darkness, against the spiritual forces of evil in the heavenly places. Therefore take up the whole armor of God, that you may be able to withstand in the evil day, and having done all, to stand firm. Stand therefore, having fastened on the belt of truth, and having put on the breastplate of righteousness, and, as shoes for your feet, having put on the readiness given by the gospel of peace. In all circumstances take up the shield of faith, with which you can extinguish all the flaming darts of the evil one; and take the helmet of salvation, and the sword of the Spirit, which is the word of God, praying at all times in the Spirit, with all prayer and supplication. To that end, keep alert with all perseverance, making supplication for all the saints.

Ephesians 6:10-18

I am walking worthy of the Lord.

So as to walk in a manner worthy of the Lord, fully pleasing to him: bearing fruit in every good work and increasing in the knowledge of God;

Colossians 1:10

I am giving God all the glory.

to the only wise God be glory forevermore through Jesus Christ! Amen.

Romans 16:27

V

Momentum

"Momentum is really a leader's best friend. Sometimes it's the only difference between winning and losing."

John Maxwell

"Benaiah chased a lion down into a pit. Then, despite the snow and slippery ground, he caught the lion and killed it."

2 Samuel 23:20-21

We were intentionally designed for community since before the beginning of time. When God made man, He noticed that Adam was lonely and needed a helpmate. But Adam didn't just need a helpmate, he needed a soulmate, a teammate. Adam needed fellowship and he needed community. Behind every great leader is a team, period. There was a parent investing in that leader as a young child; there were teachers along the way who encouraged and applauded their successes; there was a grandmother on her knees praying, plus countless others. In His sovereignty and masterful design, God made each of us for community because we are better together.

It is tragic how many people feel alone today. It is estimated that nearly 50% of Americans feel lonely. There are more people packed per square inch today than there were a hundred years ago. With technology quickly evolving and advancing, communication has never been easier or more affordable. With the helms of social media within anyone's reach, there are more ways to connect than just 20 years ago. Nonetheless, with language tools and a widely educated array of people, we must then ask ourselves why so many feel plagued with loneliness.

There is a big difference between connecting and living within community. Take, for instance, social media. Social media has become the highlight reel of our lives, where everyone posts picture-worthy moments of their lives and can even add filters to make the moment more magical. This effort does not bring people together but rather creates an underlying game of competition that is cruel at best and a dead end for the often ordinary lives we live. And where there is competition or judgment, there is isolation.

Because the moment my life doesn't match up with yours, I'm alone. Which is more connecting, two women who share the same grey and white geometrical rug? Or two women who share the deep grief and heartache of another child miscarried? It's our pain and grief, our sorrow and shattered dreams, our sinks overflowing with dirty dishes and our kids throwing their ninth fit of the hour that brings us together. It's not the perfect, but rather the messy and broken. Great leaders understand this.

Let's go back to our friend David and jump back into the story. The Israelites are trained for battle, fitted with armor and shields of the right caliber and size. They seemingly have everything they need; the weapons, the plan, the armor, the king's backing, the targeted enemy, and the ranks of each other. Yet, as the story plays out, we see that the Israelites have been paralyzed with fear for forty days and nights. What was it that they lacked? Were they fake soldiers? Had they not received proper training?

What they lacked was momentum. Momentum is defined as *"strength or force gained by motion or by a series of events."* Just because they were dressed for war and lined up for battle didn't make them ready. What wins battles is movement.

David then stepped forward, willing to do what the others weren't. He had no backing, as a matter of fact, his own blood relatives were

telling him to go home. He had no armor of his own and the king's armor was far too big and heavy for David. And his weapon? Frankly, it looked like David was bringing a Nerf gun to a sword fight. But David refused to stop, and he ran head-on against Goliath and into the enemy's camp.

I love that David didn't have to do anything different than what he had been doing his entire life. It was the same slingshot, the same smooth stones, the same God and all of heaven backing him. Once David had momentum, he didn't stop. He launched the stone, and down went Goliath. Can you imagine the rumble of the ground underneath as that massive giant finally fell? Can you hear the audible gasp of the armies as they watched in amazement? But David didn't stop there. David took Goliath's own sword, the very thing he was going to use to kill David, and cut the head of Goliath off. David killed Goliath, David cut off Goliath's head, and then David did the unthinkable…he dragged the head of the slain giant back to his camp!

I'm a visual person and ever since I was a child, I've envisioned this part of the story in "Four-K" high definition. The tendons, the severed nerves, the blood! The mere weight of the head, the adrenaline pumping through David's veins…the stench, the sweat, the heavy breathing. Why? Why did David go this far? Wasn't it enough that Goliath had been killed? Why did he use Goliath's sword to cut off his head and why did he drag the head back to camp? That's audacious!

David had momentum. David was going to finish what he started. David knew how important it was to share his success, or victory rather, with his team. Did the Israelites help David? Not really. Did they cheer him on? Not from what we can gather. Did they do anything worthwhile to contribute to the winning of this battle? No. The Israelites played pretend soldier for forty-days and it wasn't until David showed up with some cheese and crackers that things began to shift. So knowing this, it's even more peculiar why David would expend more energy and strength dragging back a bloody head to camp. David, like all great leaders, understood that his success was just a tiny part of a bigger success story. David needed to bring back the tangible evidence of that victory because he knew there were grown men in that army who had been held captive and paralyzed by their own fear for far too long.

How many people have been held back from their own destinies because of their paralyzing fear? Every single one of us. Great leaders can recognize this, show us how it's done, and then bring the victory back to camp. This not only boosts morale but brings people together and inspires them to chase down their own giants. That's the hidden power of momentum. As you keep moving and leading and serving and growing, you grow stronger and God begins using you to awaken those of us who have been playing pretend soldier for far too long in this epic, cosmic battle in the heavenlies between the forces of good and the forces of evil.

Who are the ones in your camp? Who is under your care, supervision, and leadership? How are you allowing the victories to go beyond personal to communal? God designed us for community, even leaders. Don't forget your team when you've made the big landing; thank your people, inspire them that they too can do it, and never forget that we are better together. David knew this. I don't know what was more impactful for the rest of their histories - Goliath being slain or fearful Israelites being awoken from their slumber into a world full of possibilities with, in and through God.

VI

Humility

"True humility is not thinking less of yourself; it is thinking of yourself less."

C.S. Lewis

TARA LEE DAVIS

"Whoever exalts himself will be humbled, and whoever humbles himself will be exalted."

Matthew 23:12

I've been reading the book of Job in my chronological Bible reading plan, and I'm struck. Job, a man of God whom God Himself describes as "*...There is no one on earth like him; he is blameless and upright, a man who fears God and shuns evil.*" (Job 1:8) Yet, Job began with the age-old question that we've all unashamedly asked again and again: "Why do bad things happen to good people?"

We've all been there, shaking angry fists at God as though He's missed the mark in some way. And Job's account of senseless suffering graciously hands us the largest portion of humble pie that we've needed, yet so adamantly resisted. Job questions, he wrestles, he mourns deeply, and yet he lands at who God is, and how God is everything we are not: good, pure, holy, right, and faithful in all things.

Isaiah 64:6 sums it up clearly; "*We are all infected and impure with sin. When we display our righteous deeds, they are nothing but filthy rags. Like autumn leaves, we wither and fall, and our sins sweep us away like the wind.*" In Job 38-41, God answers Job. And He answers Job by asking questions, questions that acknowledge the power, might, sovereignty and wisdom of God. This is something we need to be reminded of again and again, especially as leaders.

Great leaders acknowledge that every good and perfect gift is from God. The only good they see in another human being points back to their Creator, the goodness of God. Great leaders are humble, acknowledging that had it not been for the goodness and faithfulness of God, they would not be where they are today. *"Every good and perfect gift is from above, coming down from the Father of the heavenly lights, who does not change like shifting shadows."* (James 1:17) As a leader, your team is a gift. Your influence is a gift. Your skills and assets are a gift. Your wisdom is a gift. The very breath in your lungs is a gift. Every single good thing is a gift from God alone.

Great leaders also recognize that everything they need to lead well is given to them by God. What do you think Noah first thought when God asked him to build the ark? There were no hardware stores in the area, no power tools, no tutorial videos that can be referenced online, nothing. And yet, did God give Noah everything he needed to accomplish the task? Of course, He did. Did God provide a fattened ram for Abraham when God asked him to sacrifice his son? Did God give David the wisdom he needed to approach Goliath? Did God give Mary the grace she needed to carry a child out of wedlock and pure innocence, having never been pregnant before? Did God give Daniel the strength he needed when fasting? Was God enough for Job to endure when he lost everything?

The resounding answer, again and again, is yes and amen, because that is who He is! "*God is not human, that He should lie, not a human being, that He should change His mind. Does He speak and not act? Does He promise and not fulfill?*" (Numbers 23:19). Great leaders remain humble, knowing that without God in the front leading the way and in the mix of it all, it's all impossible and worthless, a mere chasing after the wind.

It's interesting how vital clothing is in our everyday lives. For some, it's a minimum necessity while for others it's a hobby, a culture, a way of life. There are two distinct times within Scripture that we are told to clothe ourselves. We are commanded in Ephesians 6 to clothe ourselves with the armor of God. And then in Colossians 3:12 and in 1 Peter 5:5, we are told to clothe ourselves with humility. As Christians, and especially as Christian leaders, we are to look like Jesus, sound like Jesus, and even smell like Jesus! But we cannot do this without first being clothed with the humility of Christ.

Humility is simply freedom from pride or arrogance. We get the clearest example of humility from Jesus Himself when Matthew 20:28 says this of Him; *"Just as the Son of Man did not come to be served, but to serve, and to give His life as a ransom for many."* So if Jesus, the very son of God, did not consider equality with God as something to be obtained, how much more should you and I walk in humility before God and before man? As C.S. Lewis has so brilliantly said, "Humility is not thinking less of yourself; but rather thinking of yourself less often." And here's the big deal about great leaders clothed in humility: they look like Jesus and live like Jesus and most importantly, lead like Jesus.

I love David's humility in this account. You see it long before you see what's coming. And that's how humility works. Humility is a daily discipline, and the fool who waits for victory to practice humility is doomed for failure. Long before the victory takes place, David gives credit to God for all of the times that God has proved Himself faithful to David. David, clothed in humility, knows and understands that any good found in him is only because of God.

> *"The Lord who rescued me from the claws of the lion and the bear will rescue me from this Philistine!" Saul finally consented. "All right, go ahead," he said. "And may the Lord be with you!"* 1 Samuel 17:37

David did not need Saul's vote of confidence because his confidence was completely in God, and in who God called him to be! And any of us can walk humbly before Him when we can embrace those truths. David points back again and again to the countless times that God had helped him in every situation, that's what humility does. Humility doesn't mean that we think less of ourselves, it just means we think of ourselves a whole lot less. That's the beauty of humility, it fixes our eyes where they need to be fixed in all things, and that is on Jesus.

VII

Cheese and Crackers

"Hardships often prepare ordinary people for an extraordinary destiny."

C.S. Lewis

> **"Only fear the LORD and serve him faithfully with all your heart. For consider what great things he has done for you."**
>
> **1 Samuel 12:24**

Nobody is asking you to be God. You have never been nor will you ever be God. The world does not spin on your axis; you are owed nothing. This is the bloodline of great leaders. David expected nothing, but he also didn't make himself a trophy out of his personal tragedies. There's not a hint of bitterness that no one acknowledged his anointing. There's not a shade of resentment that his big brothers were trying to shoo him back home. A leadership position or title does not make you a god; in fact, if leading like the greatest leader of all time, your leadership is simply an incredible opportunity to serve the ones around you.

David didn't have the biggest bow and arrow in the land. He didn't have the greatest following and certainly wasn't voted the "Favorite" among his family. Yet that didn't prevent David from being everything that God created and called him to be. It was as simple as cheese and crackers. David's father asked him to take the cheese and crackers and to check on his brothers at war. David did just that - he was faithful. David didn't keep an inventory of his life. He was just faithful.

Finally, great leaders understand that the battle ultimately belongs to the Lord. This seems like a trivial point to include here, but the effect of embracing this as truth shifts everything. Your position determines your perspective and your perspective changes everything about how you live your life. Understanding that the battle belongs to the Lord removes all the pressure from you and allows you to merely live. And when great leaders simply live their lives, God is able to use them and rewrite the history books in and through their everyday lives. David knew that the battle ultimately belonged to God, and that took all of the pressure off and instead allowed God to shine in and through him!

Then David said to the Philistine, "You come to me with a sword and with a spear and with a javelin, but I come to you in the name of the LORD of hosts, the God of the armies of Israel, whom you have defied. This day the LORD will deliver you into my hand, and I will strike you down and cut off your head. And I will give the dead bodies of the host of the Philistines this day to the birds of the air and to the wild beasts of the earth, that all the earth may know that there is a God in Israel, and that all this assembly may know that the LORD saves not with sword and spear. For the battle is the LORD's, and he will give you into our hand." 1 Samuel 17:45-47

What are you doing with the cheese and crackers you've been given? Obedience always carves the path to the slain giants. Be faithful, quick to obey. Quit chasing the big thing, rather do the small thing and do it well.

VIII

Reflection Questions

TARA LEE DAVIS

I: Vision

What is your vision?

_____

_____

_____

_____

What is your biggest dream?

_____

_____

_____

_____

Who is sharing that dream with you?

What do you struggle to see?

Do you have a shared vision?

_____

_____

_____

_____

Do you struggle to share your vision, and if so, why?

_____

_____

_____

_____

What from your past can fuel you for your today?

_____

_____

_____

_____

What decisions are you actively making today to impact your tomorrow?

_____

_____

_____

_____

How do you factor in your team, or your tribe, when making decisions?

_____

_____

_____

_____

How is God wanting to refine your vision?

_____

_____

_____

_____

What blurs your vision?

_____

_____

_____

_____

What helps to clarify your vision?

_____

_____

_____

_____

II: Insecurity

What are your 3 biggest insecurities?

_____

_____

_____

_____

Where did those insecurities begin?

_____

_____

_____

_____

How do those insecurities hinder you as a leader?

_____

_____

_____

_____

How have others limited you in your leadership?

_____

_____

_____

_____

How might you be limiting others under your leadership?

_____

_____

_____

_____

Who is God to you?

_____

_____

_____

_____

What characteristics of God do you struggle to believe to be true?

_____

_____

_____

_____

What does courage look like to you?

_____

_____

_____

_____

When was a time when you were courageous?

___

___

___

___

When was a time you were paralyzed by fear?

___

___

___

___

How is God wanting you to step out in courage as a leader?

_____

_____

_____

_____

What insecurities can you replace with the truth of God's Word?

Write them out below.

_____

_____

_____

_____

III: Advancing

If you could measure your faith, what would that look like today?

_____

_____

_____

_____

What do you struggle to believe, specifically about God and in yourself as a leader?

_____

_____

_____

_____

What did your first step of faith look like?

_____

_____

_____

_____

What is the next step that God is asking you to take that you're ignoring?

_____

_____

_____

_____

What makes it difficult for you step out in faith to what God is calling you to?

_____

_____

_____

_____

What are your biggest fears as a leader?

_____

_____

_____

_____

What opportunities are right in front of you?

_____

_____

_____

_____

What opportunities do you wish were in front of you?

_____

_____

_____

_____

What are the biggest motivating factors for you to keep moving ahead?

_____

_____

_____

_____

What opportunities are you giving your team to grow and learn in?

_____

_____

_____

_____

How does your action, or lack thereof, affect the ones around you?

_____

_____

_____

_____

What keeps you from acting and growing as a leader?

_____

_____

_____

_____

IV: Identity

Define yourself in 3 sentences.

_____

_____

_____

_____

Who do you wish you were?

_____

_____

_____

_____

What shapes and influences your identity the most?

_____

_____

_____

_____

How have others defined you? How did that make you feel?

_____

_____

_____

_____

What truths from God's Word define who you are?

_____

_____

_____

_____

Which is more important to you, people pleasing or God pleasing?

_____

_____

_____

_____

How has pleasing people fallen short of pleasing God?

_____

_____

_____

_____

Do you trust what God asks of you as a leader?

_____

_____

_____

_____

What do you need in order to be obedient to what God is calling you to as a leader?

_____

_____

_____

_____

How have you defined your team? How has your leadership affected their perception of their own identities?

_____

_____

_____

_____

How can you help instill truth into your team as far as identity?

_____

_____

_____

_____

If your leadership or position or title were stripped from you, would you be okay? Why or why not?

_____

_____

_____

_____

V: Momentum

Who are unsung heroes on your team?

_____

_____

_____

_____

What makes your team great? Or what could make your team better?

_____

_____

_____

_____

Who influenced you and helped shape you as a leader? Who speaks into your life now and holds you accountable, challenging you to keep growing and learning?

_____

_____

_____

_____

What does community look like to you?

_____

_____

_____

_____

Would you rather be in community or do you prefer to fly solo? Why?

_____

_____

_____

_____

How has your community helped shape you for the better?

_____

_____

_____

_____

What are the key elements, or non-negotiables, for your community?

_____

_____

_____

_____

What have been your greatest successes? Your greatest failures?

_____

_____

_____

_____

What are the greatest challenges of community for you?

_____

_____

_____

_____

What do you contribute to your community to make it better?

_____

_____

_____

_____

How do your weaknesses affect your community?

_____

_____

_____

_____

Is it easy for you to share successes with your community? Why or why not?

_____

_____

_____

_____

VI: Humility

What does humility look like to you?

_____

_____

_____

_____

Why is humility such a struggle, especially for leaders?

_____

_____

_____

_____

What are gifts in your life that you recognize God has given to you?

_____

_____

_____

_____

Do you attribute your success as a leader to yourself? Your education or experience? Or to God? Please explain.

_____

_____

_____

_____

How has God been faithful to you?

_____

_____

_____

_____

What has God given you specifically for your role in this season as a leader?

_____

_____

_____

_____

Are you being a good steward of what He has given you, why or why not?

_____

_____

_____

_____

Is it possible to walk in humility and confidence at the same time? Why or why not?

_____

_____

_____

_____

When you are no longer on this earth, how do you want to be remembered?

_____

_____

_____

_____

What is the primary goal of your life?

_____

_____

_____

_____

What would it look like in your everyday life if you lived like Jesus?

_____

_____

_____

_____

Who is a leader that you look up to and why do you look up to them?

_____

_____

_____

_____

VII: Cheese and Crackers

What kind of pressure do you feel as a leader?

_____

_____

_____

_____

How do you determine what expectations are from God versus what is from man?

_____

_____

_____

_____

What are your daily cheese and crackers?

How are you being faithful in your everyday life?

How are you not being faithful in your everyday life?

_____

_____

_____

_____

What battles are you currently facing?

_____

_____

_____

_____

How are you using your leadership for the good of others?

_____

_____

_____

_____

How do you lead in such a way that reflects that battle belonging to the Lord?

_____

_____

_____

_____

What makes it difficult for you to surrender?

How does God want to grow you as a leader?

Do you find yourself chasing something bigger than your everyday life?

_____

_____

_____

_____

How could God rewrite the history books through your everyday, ordinary life?

_____

_____

_____

_____

A Letter

Dear Weary One,

I see you. I see you taking hit after hit, getting knocked down and the enemy taunting you by whispering the count in your ear, waiting for you to tap out. You didn't sign up for this, I know. You didn't know the price you'd end up paying would be so steep. The battle scars that bleed deep and the way the arrows have punctured your lungs, causing every deep exhale to feel like the shallowest inhale.

You've lost friends along the way, some of the best. Some never crawled out of their foxholes of fear, some turned and ran away from the victory they were so close to. Others engaged in friendly fire, forgetting who the true enemy is. Yet here you are, running head-on into the enemy's camp. You were hardwired, created and designed for this epic war. You have every single thing you need to not only live in victory but to lead the ones around you to triumph. There are lives hanging in the balance and all of heaven is chanting your name. You need only believe.

Shh…be still now. Can you see the finish line? Push through, love boldly, serve relentlessly, give freely, lead joyously. Warriors are crafted in the fire. The only way to pure victory is through the refining fire. I am backing you, praying for you night and day. I will never stop believing in you, I will never stop calling you into greatness and pursuing you for this, yes this, is your destiny. You were created to be Mine, and in Me, you are complete. Fearfully and wonderfully made, the head and not the tail, an overcomer and not overcome.

Chin up champ, we are in this together and with Me at your side, nothing is impossible. The blood, sweat, and tears will be worth it all in the end when you stand before Me face to face. Just believe! The next Goliath awaits while everyone shrinks back in fear but you. You and I run head on into the enemy's camp to take back what the enemy has stolen because we are better together. You were made for this! Savage warrior, untamed by human standards, forcefully advancing My Kingdom, the Kingdom of Heaven, on this spinning blue dot of a planet.

All is not lost! Lead on brave warrior! I go before you.

-Abba

ABOUT THE AUTHOR: TARA LEE DAVIS

Reading, writing, and speaking gives Tara life. Having spent nearly a decade wandering from the heart of God and into a life of bondage, it was the love of Jesus which would ultimately set her free. Her story of redemption, freedom, and new life is woven into every facet of her writing.

Tara is a gifted storyteller, using everyday examples, raw life lessons, and humor to reach hearts. Her passion is Jesus, her gift is storytelling, and her life purpose is simple: to make much of Jesus.

www.ingramcontent.com/pod-product-compliance
Lightning Source LLC
Chambersburg PA
CBHW060331050426
42449CB00011B/2721